To _Mrs. Dolly Adams_

From _Mrs. Ada Tyree Hyche_

Thanks for what you give and who you are!

Date _January 1999_

Birmingham, Alabama

An Appreciation Book
FOR THE PASTOR'S

Wife

Carolyn Williford

Harold Shaw Publishers

Wheaton, Illinois

Scripture quotations are taken from GOD'S WORD, a copyrighted work of God's Word to the Nations Bible Society. All rights reserved.

ISBN 0-87788-609-1

Library of Congress Cataloging-In-Publication Data

Williford, Carolyn.
    An appreciation book for the pastor's wife / by Carolyn Williford.
       p.   cm.
    ISBN 0-87788-609-1
    1. Spouses of clergy.   I. Title.
    BV4395.W56 1998
    253'.22—dc21

                                          98-27614
                                           CIP

Edited by Elizabeth Cody Newenhuyse

Cover design by David LaPlaca

02 01 00 99 98

10 9 8 7 6 5 4 3 2 1

FOR CRAIG

The lovable guy who made me a pastor's wife

 *What's Inside*

PART 4

Springs of Refreshment

PART 5

Taste and See!

Acknowledgments

My sincere thanks to my friends, the contributing pastors' wives who shared their stories; to Elizabeth Cody Newenhuyse, for her belief in and work on this project; and finally to Polly, for her many contributions and her wonderful love.

PART 1

Open These Gifts First!

You know that the hard work you do
for the Lord is not pointless.
—1 Corinthians 15:58

A Note of Thanks

Have you ever thought of yourself as a gift?

You are, you know. You're a gift to your church, to your husband, to your children, to your friends, to all those you minister to. Think about it.

You are a gift for coaching twenty squirming preschoolers through "Away in a Manger" in the Sunday school Christmas program . . . for patiently listening to the reminiscences of an elderly saint . . . for opening your home and heart to a basement full of energetic teenagers.

You are a gift for juggling your many roles as wife, mother, friend, employee, woman of God . . . for your commitment to the ministry life through all its ups and downs . . . for your heart for God.

It isn't always easy—but know that your faithfulness does not go unnoticed. That fragrant offering is appreciated by so many. Most important, you are appreciated by the audience of One: our God. Stop

Here, then, are stories of empathy, encouragement, hope through hard times, and a liberal dose of humor (because some days you just have to laugh). Here, too, are stories and reflections from fellow ministry wives: I'm calling them *Heart to*

Heart. I hope that, by the time you've finished the book, you'll feel refreshed and affirmed.

So now, take a moment for *you*. Put the kids to bed, climb into your favorite robe, and fix yourself a cup of instant cappuccino. Let the answering machine get the phone. You've got a book—a book for and about you—to read.

God's Gift of Growth

Remember some of the pastors' wives in your childhood church? Your life and approach to ministry is undoubtedly quite different from theirs. Chances are you have a part-time or full-time job; or, if you are at home, you're more likely to be teaching your kids than hosting elegant dinners. If you have kids at home, your husband is probably a much more involved dad than his father was. Both of you may be re-evaluating the priorities of family and ministry, searching for new and creative ways to make sure your children aren't turned off to Christ because of their experiences as preacher's kids. You want to be perceived as a unique individual, complete in Christ.

How is all this making a difference? Many of you—us, because I've struggled with all these issues—are more selective about involvement at church. Most significantly, ministry itself is being changed by our desires. Congregations don't always expect the pastor's wife to play the piano and plan vacation Bible school. Dads don't want to be away from their families night after night. And pastoral families are calling for a holistic approach to ministry in which their children are not merely uninvolved and possibly resentful bystanders. Instead, Mom and Dad are packing up the kids, taking them on everything from trips across town to short-term missions trips overseas.

We're responding differently from previous generations to the demands of ministry, questioning more, searching for new definitions of what it means to serve Christ and grow in him. And that's healthy, but, as we plow new ground, we create new challenges for ourselves.

God has gifted you with a wealth of traits and talents; working those out authentically takes courage, especially when you're traveling through new and uncertain territory. Need motivation for the challenge? That's the way we grow in Christ. It all comes down to this: what does God want *you* to be, my friend?

The Gift of the Tumbledown Parsonage

What's *your* worst-place-we-ever-lived-in story? Bet I can top it.

Take the first parsonage we lived in. Now, *that* was a microcosm of the ministry lifestyle. It was, first of all, right next door to the church. Craig checked it out with a trustee, giving it a quick look before we would come back to go through it again. Curious about our living arrangements, I asked Craig about the house.

He was vague. Not a good sign. A new tactic was needed. Groping for specifics and fretting about curtains, I inquired about the number of windows in the master bedroom. "Let's see . . . one, two, three, um . . . yeah, it's seven. Definitely seven."

"Craig. No bedroom has seven windows."

"Well, this one does."

I should have known not to argue. There were indeed seven. (One of the previous owners worked for a glass factory.) During my first tour—after tiptoeing through fallen plaster and squishy carpet to view a kitchen with a sink roughly the size of the *Titanic*—the deacons said, "Well, I guess we could fix it up a little."

That was what you might call one of those "reality moments."

So how was that little parsonage a mirror of ministry? Even though that was our first full-time pastorate, I learned three things pretty quickly. It was so many years ago, but the rules haven't changed:

❖ No matter whether we're across the parking lot or across town, we still have to establish boundaries. *Rule to live by:* My whole life is not this church.

❖ What you see isn't what you get. Or, what you're told isn't necessarily how it's going to be. From the outside, that house didn't look too bad. But from the inside, it was definitely a handyman's paradise.

At the same time, those deacons really came through. New carpet, new paint, new wallpaper (new walls, for that matter), and a thorough cleaning made a tremendous difference. (The sink, however, remained.) *Rule to live by:* Trust in God, but keep your expectations in check.

❖ That house had problems galore: the furnace was wheezing its last gasps, the shades flapped when a breeze blew, and the roof leaked. But the joy that we knew in that little home was indescribable. Sure, I remember all its foibles; but I also recall the laughter, praise, prayers, and songs that echoed through those rooms. *Rule to live by:* We must strive not to be blinded by the hard and painful times; they will be glaring in their intensity. Instead, let us search for the joys—they will be the gifts of eternal value.

How to Give to Others and Not Give Out

I'm sure you're a good giver. But are you a good receiver? For many of us, it isn't easy to receive—or even consider our own needs. And yet, while we're serving others, we need to be aware of those needs. If you're one of those Martha-like servants, here are nine gifts you need to give yourself.

- Time with God
- Time alone
- Time with your husband
- Time with family
- Time with friends
- Forgiving yourself when you fail
- Being who God created you to be
- Laughter
- Perspective

And let's not forget the greatest gift of all. I've saved the best for last—read on.

And the Greatest Gift Is . . .

Does the wonder of the gift ever strike you as it does me?
Jesus! The greatest of all gifts, for he gave his very life.

Many times I skim over that truth, thinking *Yes* with my head. Other times, I embrace it, affirming *Yes!* with my soul.

Jesus defined himself for us in so many ways, possibly to help our finite minds better grasp the enormousness of what he was actually giving. Peter's bold declaration "You are the Messiah, the Son of the Living God!" (Matt. 16:16) lays the foundation for the rock on which Christ says he will build his church (v. 18). This fulfills Zechariah's promise: "From [Judah] will come a cornerstone" (10:4). And what encouragement we receive from reading Jesus' promise: "I am the light of the world. Whoever follows me will have a life filled with light and will never live in the dark" (John 8:12).

While confronting the Samaritan woman in John 4:1-26, Christ offers her "living water," a drink that guarantees that those who partake will "never become thirsty again." When he spoke of "true bread from heaven" (John 6:32) and the people asked him to bring them that heavenly bread, Jesus replied, "I am the bread of life" (v. 35).

He gives us gifts that are . . .

✝ *Strengthening and touchable, like a rock.* As pastors' wives, we can feel those expectations to always be strong for others. But sometimes we desperately need something solid to grab hold of. We need a Rock to cling to.

✝ *Illuminating and revealing, like light.* Then there are times we want to shout, "Believe it or not, folks, we don't have all the answers!" We stumble in the darkness just like everyone else; we need Light to guide our way.

✝ *Refreshing and replenishing, like water.* After a season of stressful and demanding ministry, we can feel dry, depleted, empty. We give and give until we have nothing left to give. We need refilling from the Living Water.

✝ *Nourishing and substantial, like bread.* It's easy to get caught up in the superficial—shallow relationships, busyness without purpose. But, like the way we feel a couple of hours after a breakfast of bagel and coffee, we hunger for something more lasting. We need nourishment from the Bread of Life.

Touch, behold, drink, eat . . . and enjoy!

PART 2

In the Shelter of the Rock

I love you, O Lord, my strength. The Lord is my rock and
my fortress and my Savior, my God, my rock in whom I take refuge,
my shield, and the strength of my salvation, my stronghold.

—Psalm 18:1-2

Remember the story of the child who was afraid of the storm and asked for a hug, saying she needed "God with skin on," instead of the reassurance of an (to her) abstract Father? The following stories are, in a sense, God's "hugs." I hope that in these reflections and reminiscences you'll find spiritual strengthening—rocks to cling to.

My Rock Collection

Some years you might feel as if the foundations under you have started to crumble. We had a year like that, a year when everything we thought was solid fell away. When my husband, Craig, was released from his job due to a financial crisis at the college where he taught, the very earth beneath my feet seemed to have dissolved into nothingness. No paycheck? No security? What would we do?

What I did was struggle—with God. I felt abandoned, thrown away, rejected. All we wanted to do was serve him and minister. Didn't God want us anymore? I argued and pleaded and railed, but, of course, it didn't solve anything. One morning I came to him with a humbled spirit, reflecting on the role of faith in my life: was it operative only in the good times? What about the bad? Out of the struggle came a desire to recommit myself and our family to God and to help our two sons grow in their faith through this difficult time.

The next thing I did was collect rocks—five of them, to be exact. One for each of us, the dog included. That evening we sat in a circle on the floor around our wedding candle, holding those rocks in our hands, rubbing them, feeling their solidity. "Compared to our faith in God, though, these rocks are nothing," we told our sons (and ourselves). "These stones could be crushed or blown away or lost in an ocean. But God's promises to us are secure forever. Nothing can destroy them—nothing!"

When we placed our rocks around the base of that candle, we built an altar like Joshua was told to do, a family altar that would forever be a reminder of God's faithfulness to us. Then every night after that we lit the candle and waited for God to work. In time, he did, and we moved on to the next ministry, but not before we gathered around our altar to thank and praise him with tears of joy.

That was more than ten years ago, but when you walk into our family room you'll still spot a yellowing, shrunken candle with five ordinary-looking stones at its base. It has weathered two more moves, been lit for countless family devotions and holidays, and seen us through hard and happy times. And each one of us (well, except the dog) has picked up one of those rocks when we needed a comfort, a reminder, a touchable representation of strength—of Christ.

When those times of crisis come, here is a prayer that has helped me and may encourage you as well: *Dearest Father, may I always look to you as the source of true strength, recognizing that this is one of your treasured gifts to me. And may I give myself the gift of sometimes being weak or needy or even lacking in faith. For how could I grasp the Rock in my hands, if mine were already filled?*

Touched by a Saint

When our daughter was an infant, my husband was paying regular calls on a homebound, elderly woman in our church. She lived in an apartment above a store in a working-class city neighborhood, up a rickety fire escape. She hardly ever went out, except when she got rides to church. She was blind and suffered from a variety of other disabling conditions—but she was also a real saint who deeply appreciated my husband's regular visits.

Our church had a lot of older people who enjoyed seeing the pastor *and* his wife on afternoon calls. Having a new baby (born in the winter) had curtailed my activities in that area, but by the time Amanda was a few months old, my husband and I agreed we should bring her along on selected visits. So one day the whole family went to see Myrtle. We climbed those worrisome steps, me clutching the baby, and Myrtle let us in. She offered us seats in her neat apartment, moving slowly. Then my husband said, "Oh, Myrtle, we brought Amanda—our new baby."

"You did?" she exclaimed. (Her only family was a nephew in the area.)

"Yes. Would you like to hold her?"

"Could I?"

Carefully I put Amanda into her waiting arms. Even though Myrtle was sightless and childless, she knew how to welcome an infant onto her lap—it must be an instinct all we women possess. Amanda, clearly comfortable, smiled into Myrtle's unseeing eyes—and then reached up her hands to explore the fragile, paper-flower elderly skin. Myrtle broke into a delighted smile as she returned the favor, touching our daughter's downy hair and velvet cheek.

I watched with tears in my eyes, reflecting on how these two were, in a sense, bumping into each other on the path to heaven—one new to earthly life, the other gradually letting go of it. This is a real privilege of the pastorate: to *be with* people at various life stages. My daughter won't remember the touch of those fragile hands, but perhaps part of her baby spirit was touched by the presence of a saint.

—*E. C. N.*

Is the Turkey a Better Buy?

Don't you love those annual board meetings where they decide whether your husband is worthy of his hire and discuss his salary for the upcoming year? It feels like sorting through packages of raw hamburger at the meat counter: *Is it a good bargain? Are we getting our money's worth? Can we get more for less? Is the turkey a better buy?*

After the meeting you might hear snatches of positive and negative comments, particularly if the one guy who's been on the Trustee Board since the Eisenhower Administration—and whose concept of pastoral salaries was frozen around 1958—decides to offer his view. That invariably filters back. In complete and rich detail. After all these years in ministry, receiving a salary from the church still brings out those same uncomfortable feelings: we're on display. Exposed. Vulnerable. *Owned*.

All I know is this: I can't allow myself to look at that paycheck as a measure of worth. Long ago, my husband said something very wise: if I judge my worth only by what I can produce through a paid job, then I've made myself of less value than those mere things. A paycheck puts a dollar amount on our heads. It announces,

"You, insignificant person that you are (especially in light of professional ballplayers' salaries), are worth this measly amount."

There's no way around it. I've got to reject that pattern of thinking. I have to make a choice: to decide to listen to the thank-you notes and cards that come our way instead; to hear the kind words that say, "You bless us, you enrich us, we are grateful for you. Thank you for teaching me, challenging me, stimulating me, and fanning the flames for Christ within me." You can't put a dollar amount on that.

Still . . . maybe just this once . . . could this year's board *try?*

Oh Boy, More "Footprints"!

Over the course of the year the "Footprints" poem (do I have to recite it to you?) first became popular, my husband and I probably received ten gifts of plaques, pictures, a clock, and even a cross-stitched version of the poem. Each and every time, we would open the gift and look up at the giver, and she would have such an expectant look—tears in her eyes sometimes— knowing how moved we were going to be by this poem and assuming she was the first to share it. As you can imagine, it became a bit more difficult to act surprised each successive time, even though we did appreciate the sentiments behind the gift. Eventually we received so many that I remodeled our private bath in "Early Footprints" with all our mementos in there!

A few years ago a pastoral couple who are dear friends invited us for a beautiful dinner—complete with candles, china, the works. And then they presented us with a beautifully wrapped gift with kind words about how much our friendship had meant to them and that they had chosen this gift because it expressed their hearts so well. My husband opened it, and there it was—"Footprints" again, only this time as a note holder and matching pen. He and I looked at each other, absolutely speechless, until our friends burst into laughter. We had forgotten that we had told them about our "treasured" collection, and they simply couldn't pass up the chance to do it to us . . . once again.

—L. P.

Habakkuk, Whining, and Us

If you have kids, this will sound familiar. If you *were* a kid, this will sound familiar. "Why not?" "But I *want* to . . . he gets to." "It's not fair!" Or, better yet: "She's touching me." "He's bothering me." "She *looked* at me!" Kids are professionals at whining. As a parent, I did my best to ignore it, but nothing ever seemed to stop it. I suppose it's simply part of being a parent to listen to that incessant whining—when all along you knew what was best for your children.

Suppose God feels the same way sometimes?

Several years ago I was reading through the minor prophets for my devotions when I came to the book of Habakkuk. Habakkuk, you'll recall, was a contemporary of Jeremiah, a man of deep faith. But he also was quite human—and therefore much like all of us—in that he came to God with several complaints. As a matter of fact, he argued with God quite vigorously over the injustices of his day—and God's rather obvious lack of action to resolve such matters. "How long, O Lord, am I to cry for help, but you will not listen?" (1:2) he cries. From that beginning, Habakkuk persistently gripes to God about the prosperity of the wicked while he,

Habakkuk, suffers. "Why do you keep watching treacherous people? Why are you silent when wicked people swallow those who are more righteous than they are?" (1:13) he demands. Sometimes the injustices of this world, and especially those that sneak right into my home, are too much. So I, like Habakkuk, lament, gripe, complain, whine—whatever you want to call it—to God. At one time I probably felt guilty about it and cut myself off, shaming myself into silence before my Lord. But you know what? That same *spirit* of whining was still there; I had just driven it underground. Time for a new tactic.

That's where Habakkuk really hit home. He let it all out before God. A child of God who feels free to question, to express his or her emotions and attitudes, to even whine to God, has an open and real relationship.

Habakkuk's whining, as it turns out, was not in vain. Note the last three verses. Habakkuk gets specific about his beefs by actually listing out all his troubles: "Even if the fig tree does not bloom . . . vines have no grapes . . . fields yield no food . . . sheep pen is empty and the stalls have no cattle . . . *even then* [italics added] I will be happy with the Lord" (3:17-18).

Here we see the great difference between those who find contentment and those who don't. Habakkuk knows that the secret of contentment lies in the ability to be completely honest with God—not for God's benefit, but for ours—and in having the strength of character to then move on to the next needed step: faith, whatever the circumstances.

Advice for Modern Habakkuks

Habakkuk's list of troubles moved me to create my own. I had a great time moaning when I wrote:

Even though
— the money from our income tax refund is gone (a new transmission wiped it out)
— the car breaks down (said transmission)
— the money in our savings account is almost gone
— we can't go out to eat (I told you I was whining)
— a job offer didn't work out
— we can't take a vacation
— we can't buy a house (we were in a rental, and an ugly one at that)

Even though all these happen, still . . .

— I will exult in the Lord
— I will rejoice in the God of my salvation.

Habakkuk concludes with one last encouraging reminder: "The Lord Almighty is my strength. He makes my feet like those of a deer. He makes me walk on the mountains" (3:19). I've seen Colorado bighorn sheep amble along mountain paths—incredibly treacherous ledges which made me shake my head in amazement as I followed their progress. And I wondered to myself, *"Why on earth would they do that? Why would they place themselves in such danger?"* In some instinctive way, those sheep trusted their ability to negotiate the precipices.

That's the image that God presents in this passage: security, a strong foothold no matter what precipice we're clinging to. When we *choose* to rejoice—no matter what—we, too, will lightly scale the high places.

Go ahead. Start your list.

Heart to Heart

A Last Conversation

When my mother was fighting a battle with cancer, I asked God to give me some insight to know when to leave our home in New York and go to be with her. I had called the doctor several times, asking for his wisdom, and finally had abandoned the decision to God to give me help to know. I called my sister, also a pastor's wife who lived thirty miles away, and we both had the strong feeling we should make our way down to Virginia. Because she was several months pregnant, my sister decided to travel by plane. I didn't feel our budget could handle that expense; therefore, I planned to leave the end of that week and drive down alone.

The following day a friend from the church dropped in to see me. She knew my mother was not doing well and, having lost her own mother many years before, was sensitive to my situation. We chatted at length about the mundane. But when she stood to leave she took my hand, pressed something into my palm and said, "I had this set aside with nothing in mind for it. I would like you to have it. Please use this to fly to see your mother. Sit by her side as long as you can." With a hug, she left. In my palm was a one hundred-dollar bill!

My sister and I flew to Virginia and were met at the airport by my father. His opening question to us was, "How did you know to come now?" The doctor had visited my mother that morning and unexpected surgery was planned early the next day. As the day progressed, we had precious time to talk and listen as Mom shared her love for us and for the Lord. She told us how she longed to stay with us and see our histories and families unfold. But even more important than that, she shared, was whatever God wanted for her.

That was our last conversation before my mom went to be with the Lord. I was able to have that time because of a gift given by a friend—and a Friend who knew the timetable of which we had no knowledge.

—P. J.

PART 3

When God Turns On a Light

Once you lived in the dark, but now the Lord has filled you with light.
Live as children who have light. . . . Light exposes the true character
of everything because light makes everything easy to see.
—Ephesians 5:8-14

Who does windows in February, especially if you live in a northern climate? Not me. At this moment I'm looking through a dirty window. It will have to wait until spring for cleaning (no way I'm opening the window during an Ohio winter), but in the meantime, it distorts what I view. Those water spots and various smudges cloud my perspective of the sky, trees, and grass. So as I gaze out at the scene before me, I wonder, Is the sky really that gray? Is there something lying in the yard, or am I looking at a fingerprint smeared on the pane? When our windows are dirty, we're not sure what's real and what's not.

Jesus said, "I am the light of the world" (John 8:12). He is the ultimate filter, the One who defines the experiences of our lives, the One who then gives those experiences reason and purpose. Once he enters our lives as personal Savior, we then "filter" everything we see through the lens of his window, his Spirit. Even then, however, our view can be blurred by our own denial, immaturity, or just plain sin. That's why Jesus sometimes sends us those "lightbulb experiences" that make us realize, Oh, so THAT'S what he meant! Here, then, are a few stories to illumine your own spiritual window.

You Don't Have to Like Me

We all want to do so well when we're new at ministry, don't we? When Craig and I were starting out, I suppose I was something of a people-pleaser. I wanted to be a partner to Craig in his duties, and I judged that for people to accept my contributions of love, teaching, help, and friendship, I would have to please them. I assumed that, by pleasing them, they would like me; and then they would be receptive to my ministering. So, I did just about anything I could to make sure everyone—and I mean everyone—would like me.

It didn't work too well.

First of all, even though I would consider myself a fairly likeable person (come on now, don't we all think that?), I quickly discovered that everyone did not find me irresistible. As a matter of fact, it was quite obvious that there were some out there who simply didn't click with me and never would. Second, and equally painful, was the realization that I didn't like everybody in our church either. Certain people irritated me, frustrated me beyond belief, and drove me crazy!

The first revelation hurt me deeply, and the second left me feeling inadequate, guilty, and unloving as a Christian. How was I to minister to someone I didn't like? And how could I rationalize that lack of heartfelt love for someone who bugged me every time I met him or her in the hallway? (Ducking into the ladies' room to avoid an encounter didn't seem quite appropriate.)

It wasn't until years had gone by—and several miserable attempts at resolution along the way—that I finally had one of those light bulb experiences. I had to recognize and accept the difference between liking and loving someone. We're called to *love* everyone, but the Word never demands that we *like* everyone. I'd actually heard that concept years ago, but I was never able to put it to work in my life until I realized that I needed to give myself a gift. One of the best presents I've ever received, this was its essence: *I would give others the gift of not having to like me.*

Sounds pretty simple, doesn't it? Maybe so, but the moment I truly caught that principle and began to apply it in my life made a world of difference. Here's how it works:

1. A particularly annoying person moves into the sphere of our ministry.
2. I give that person the gift of not having to like me.
3. The gift works both ways: I don't have to like him or her either!
4. I am freed from the pressure to force feelings that aren't genuine.
5. Without those pressures on me, I am freed to love. As a result, I find myself feeling, if not a liking, then an understanding of that person that I did not have before.

Looking Past the Grime

I'm sure you have your own story about "The Most Unlovable Person I've Ever Had to Deal With in a Church." This is one of mine, and I'll never forget the first time that light bulb clicked on. I was in Sunday school, and right in front of me sat this particular person who had been on my "trying desperately to love/like/please prayer list." She was sharing something particularly annoying (I can't recall what it was now, but she had a tendency to be extremely controversial in her political views, and I suspect it was something on that order), and when she threw her hand up into the air to make a point, I noticed her fingernails. They were quite long, and filthy. After she finished sharing, she proceeded to pick at them, one by one.

Understand, this woman was not poor; on the contrary, she and her husband were quite wealthy. But as I stared at her back, silently wondering why on earth she would come to church unclean, the realization finally hit me: it was time to give *her* the gift of not having to like Carolyn. I pictured myself presenting this gift to the bent form in front of me—no strings, no attachments. Done. And the peace of that decision began to slowly move from my head to my heart.

It didn't happen overnight, that transformation. But it *did* happen. After continued prayer, I began to see her in a new light—through the lens of a cleaner window. Eventually, I realized that she came to church looking frazzled and messy with grimy nails—even spouting those inflammatory views—because she believed that she was not *worthy* of our love. It seemed as if she was challenging us to love her just as she was, dirty, caustic, and irritating.

I set out to prove her self-perceptions wrong. Every time I saw her, I gave her a hug. And she cuddled up to me like a child who was starving for attention. I wonder, who received more—that lonely woman, or me?

"How Is He—Really?"

Going through a personal struggle when you're a "public" figure is really hard. It was very painful for me when my dad was sick; he was ill for so long and he was in so much pain that it nearly broke my heart. Most people who knew me understood that my dad was dying, and that I was very close to him. A lot of people asked about him, which was kind—except that I soon discovered they wanted to ask merely because it was the right thing to do. Sadly, they really didn't care to know his actual condition. That was the hardest lesson for me: learning that when they asked, all they wanted to hear was, "He's doing fine." No one truly wanted to listen to my heart (including my pastor-husband's employer—that one *really* hurt). No one, that is, except for Pam.

Pam wasn't even a close friend. But we were at a get-together one evening and she asked the usual: "Kathy, how's your dad doing?" And I said he was okay, thanks. She looked at me with such kindness in her eyes and began asking questions about him; before I knew it, I had unloaded a whole truckload of how it was breaking my heart to tell him good-bye (I wasn't even out of my twenties), and she listened all the while. We crossed paths probably four or five times during his illness, and each time when Pam asked, she made the question itself a gift. I had never realized what a gift it is to offer someone your caring, undivided attention—but knew I must learn to care for others' hearts like she had cared for mine.

—K. L.

Light on a Misty Day

It's fun to go walking and look at houses—usually. Then there are other days when it isn't so fun.

I was on one of my regular morning walks, but since it was raining, Wendy (our black Labrador) and I were working our way through the subdivision instead of the woods or the park. I didn't want her to get muddy, and I was in a rotten mood. The grayness of the day and the steady downpour didn't help any. But those were surface issues; the core issue went far deeper.

I noted a crew of workmen finishing a deck on a house. *Must be nice,* I thought grudgingly. (Craig and our sons had done ours, and it took three summers before we could afford to complete it.) A brand-new car sat in another driveway. *(Wish we could have one.)* I noticed the designer "window treatments" in a third house's front room and sparkling white patio furniture on another porch. Seemed like everyone had new stuff—everyone except us.

And I resented it.

In truth, that's not like me. Sure, there are times I get little twinges of envy. But this terrible *wanting* was threatening to eat away at me. "Help me, Lord," I prayed. "Help me to understand what's going on inside of me."

We never entered ministry—obviously not!—to become rich. And as those around us prospered materially in their respective secular areas, I rejoiced with them and was able to remain content because I had a guiding reason to stay in ministry: I loved God's people and wanted to serve them.

But suddenly, on that gloomy day, I knew that particular motivation wasn't enough, wasn't working, wasn't *right*. I needed some other reason to keep at this.

Why? Because people had hurt me terribly. Tears mingled now with the rain on my cheeks. I remembered the woman who hadn't remained loyal. The board that hadn't kept its promise. The church that made money—off of us. The alleged friends who weren't there to support us in our time of greatest need.

And on and on and on. The motivation to "serve people" was actually choking off my heart, my love for this life, and ironically, my love for God's people.

As I slogged along, the answer came through the foggy mist in such clear, simple terms: I must decide to stay in ministry because I love *my God*. And I want to serve him. Yes, it works out through people, but God never fails me. People do. And when you need a reason for keeping at something that won't allow you to pay someone to put on a deck or to buy a new car, it had better be one that lasts.

What will that motivation allow you to do? See God heal a marriage; walk with a dying saint to the doorway of eternity; raise children who "catch" the value of serving people, not earning things.

I raised my teary face to the pouring rain . . . and felt his love cleanse my soul.

The Chocolate-Chip Mystery

One evening when the kids were small, we came home to find a big plate full of oatmeal/chocolate-chip cookies by our door, along with a brief, anonymous note. We were touched by the mysterious gift, and then, when we tasted the cookies, we *loved* them. I mean, they were perfect. I asked around in an effort to find out who the donor might be, but to no avail. This gift was clearly going to remain anonymous.

About four or five years later, we had a big group of college kids in our home one night. We were talking about the topic of giving, and I shared with them how kind I thought that gift had been so many years before, how much I desired the recipe, and how I had never been able to discover the "mystery baker." A couple of days later, there on my doorstep was a plate of those very same cookies. This time, though, they came with the recipe. Imagine: the person who sent the cookies the first time was around four years later and STILL chose to remain anonymous. I never did find out who it was, but she (probably she—that's sexist, I know!) lifted my spirits incredibly because of her joy of giving secretly.

—*K. L.*

All Things to All . . .

I'd love to do a scientific research project in which I'd ask church people these questions: What should a pastor's wife look like and act like? Wouldn't those answers be interesting? Sometimes I do wonder what goes through people's minds. The questions I get asked! Here's a sampling from the past:

1. Deacon Donahue: As we pass in the hallway, he says hello (that one I can handle) and then asks, "Oh, by the way, what time is the next board meeting?"
I answer: "Sorry, I don't know. You'll have to call my husband's secretary."
I think to myself: *Do I look like the official walking church calendar?*

2. Theologian Theo: As I'm rushing to meet Craig, Theo corners me in the back of the auditorium: "You know, your husband really should know that the latest hermeneutical studies show that . . . " and on and on.
   Finally I get a word in: "That's sooo interesting, Theo, but I really must run!"
   I think to myself: *Do I have a bull's-eye on my back? If you're eager to criticize, don't target me!*

3. *Disorganized Dorothy:* She spies me at the local library and immediately begins digging through her purse. "I know that form's in here somewhere. Oh, here it is. Would you please give this to your husband? He wanted it back last week. It's about the new curriculum we're using in Sunday school."

I respond: "Sure. No problem."

I think to myself: *If I say no, my husband won't get the form for another week. But by saying yes, I've indicated that I'm a delivery service. I can't win!*

Resolution for a pastor's wife: I will *not* be all things to all people. But sometimes I'll do what I must—and chuckle to myself to keep my sanity.

The Land of "What If"

We were newcomers to the church when I went to the hospital for a medical test. We had four young children at the time. The test went smoothly, but for some reason the technician came back in and did a rerun. My mind began to race ahead into the land of *what if*—a dangerous territory. By the time I returned home, my questions had turned into: What if something is seriously wrong? What if I need surgery? What if I have a debilitating disease? Who will care for my children? *What if?* It was one of those pondering-in-the-heart moments.

That afternoon an older widow on staff at the church came unexpectedly to my door. Over tea she asked if she could run something by me. She was asked to speak at a mother-daughter banquet and had chosen the story of Hannah and Samuel for her topic. She unfolded her outline to me. "Isn't it interesting," she said, "that after praying so long for this little boy, Hannah's faith in God allowed her to hand Samuel over to be raised by a man who could not adequately parent his own two children?"

I had a loving husband and family—and a generous Father who was in complete control. In that moment, I was freed from the land of *what if*.

—A. J.

PART 4

Springs of Refreshment

The Lord will continually guide you and satisfy you
even in sun-baked places. He will strengthen your bones.
You will become like a watered garden
and like a spring whose water does not stop flowing.
—Isaiah 58:11

It's a strange paradox: very often those who are in the most danger of running spiritually dry are people who are involved in "Christian work" in some way. We're busy on behalf of God, we're reading about God, we're talking about God with other believers. But even the largest of pitchers eventually runs dry. While we're filling others, we can become empty ourselves. We dare not neglect our own needs, our own thirsts.

Recently Craig and I went scuba diving. It took all the courage I could gather to trust that breathing equipment, but how exhilarating to discover the incredible beauty that lies beneath our oceans! In the instructions we received before we could practice with the equipment, I learned that our bodies are nearly 80 percent water. Amazing, isn't it? Of all the substances that make up my body—bone, muscle, tissue, fat, skin, organs, and whatever else is stuffed in there—everything feels fairly solid to me (if you can call cellulite solid). I would never have imagined that most of me was made up of water.

I think that makes Jesus' picture of himself as Living Water even more meaningful. As we drink of him, a life-giving river flows into our bodies, reaching and filling every niche, every crack, every thirsty place in us! We are cleansed, made new.

So drink up—and refresh yourself with these stories.

The Incredible Shrinking Check

When you're chronically tight for money, as many of us ministry families seem to be, financial ups and downs can really get to you. For example . . .

It was the first year that we were to get a sizable check from the government for overpayment of income taxes, and we were elated. As soon as Craig finished all the forms and announced the final figure—just over eight hundred dollars!—we began plotting how to spend it. By that spring of 1985, we had seen some pretty lean times, and we probably looked forward to that check about like the Israelites awaited entry to the Promised Land. And, like the Israelites, we were about to encounter one small barrier: we had a river to cross first.

Shortly after we'd mailed the income tax forms, our new used car began doing strange things. Again. It simply would not go above twenty miles per hour. We took it to a service station and held our breaths, hoping that the mechanic would say, "Eh, it's just a minor problem." His actual reply: we needed a new transmission.

The bill turned out to be almost exactly eight hundred dollars. When the check finally arrived, I clutched it in my hands (I wanted to at least gaze at it as long as I could) and figured we now had a whopping $1.53 to spend frivolously on ourselves. The wish list we had so hopefully come up with was tossed in the trash.

My attitude was pretty much in the trash, too. I knew that somehow, I needed to settle this with my God. I sat alone at the kitchen table, the place where I come to God to study, journal, pray. With one last deep breath of surrender, I blew my nose, took up my pen and wrote a letter that went like this:

My Lord,
I don't know why all the money must be taken, but it has been and now I must deal with that. But I realize it's an attitude choice: Do I become angry that it was "ours" and you took it away, or do I accept the fact that it was never ours and be happy that you provided the money specifically for this purpose? I can choose to be angry at you or to thank you. Please help me to live in and choose your way!

Your child,
Carolyn

Writing down my prayer helped clarify the choices I faced. Gradually God gave me the ability to view the entire experience as a gift. And I finally thanked him.

Years later, to pay capital-gains taxes we were forced to empty our savings. That time, the choice to view it as his provision was easier because of lessons from the past. After all, it's only money—we've never had any anyway!—and ultimately it all belongs to him.

In Search of
Soul Sisters

One of the things that can make life in the ministry so hard is the feeling of aloneness, the lack of intimate relationships. Our lifestyle is not always conducive to making deep connections. We tend to move more often. After being stung by a hurtful situation, we may have the tendency to protect ourselves by remaining distant from church people. And finally, there's the warning we've probably all heard: a pastor's wife should never have a close friend within the church.

I first heard that pearl at our very first church, articulated as great wisdom from a pastor's wife. I suppose I pondered that as a viable option for maybe a minute or two. And then I set about searching for an intimate female friend. God provided "Huh-Huh" (a cherished nickname that came from our son's inability to pronounce Aunt Helen). Helen was a godly mentor to me, a gift from God who filled—and still fills—some of the deepest needs of my soul.

When we moved away so that Craig could attend seminary, my heart ached to leave her. How on earth could I replace what she so lovingly gave me? In God's infinite wisdom, he didn't replace her. Instead, he provided a different type of soul-mate friend, Judy. And then later when we moved again (eventually suffering a devastating job loss), I clung to the loyalty that Diana and Carol so willingly gave. At Craig's new position, June and Jo loved and accepted me unconditionally. And now that we're back in Ohio, I've come full circle: Huh-Huh is only an hour away, and I have intimate friends at this church, too.

I know it isn't always as easy for every pastor's wife. Believe me, I recognize the incredible blessing I've received. I don't take God's part in that lightly.

At the same time, I *sought* those friendships. God helped me to recognize the thirst in my soul. I could never begin to express how those women have been small streams of the Living Water to me.

Great, you're saying. *What about me?* If you're hurting, feeling alone and friendless, know that your Best Friend cares deeply about the pain you're feeling. Every time we've moved, I've poured out my sadness to God, and I knew that God lovingly listened. I've also had friends reject me, betray confidences, desert me in times of great need. There have been times when those I thought would become lifelong friends turned out not to be a good "fit" after all. I grieved and then moved on.

My encouragement to you? Never give up in your search for intimate friends. Don't put limitations on age (some of my closest friends are older, some are much younger), location (e-mail and phone calls make long distance intimacy possible), race (shouldn't racial reconciliation begin with God's people?), economic levels, or culture. She's out there. *Find her.*

Books for the Thirsty Soul

*M*any pastors' wives are great readers. When I asked friends to talk about "the best gifts I ever gave myself," many of them mentioned reading. Here's what a couple said:

When the criticisms at church are too much, when the kids are driving me crazy, when my work seems endless and "the hurrier I go the behinder I get"—that is the time to become completely absorbed in another world, a world with characters who become my friends, my teachers, my guides to another time and place. I've traveled to other planets with Madeleine L'Engle, climbed through a wardrobe with C. S. Lewis, and learned to care about a marooned dog and strutting rooster in the chicken yard of Walt Wangerin's imagination. With each intimate visit with those and countless other characters, I've learned more about relationships, about myself, about

God. When people ask me if I'm currently reading a book, I generally reply, "I'm breathing, so I'm reading!"

—S. W.

I had an aunt whom I dearly loved; she was passionate about reading, and I think she passed her love of books on to my sisters and me. She was single, lived in New York City, and she spent her vacation with us each year. I simply adored her. I remember her not only reading to me, but telling me that if I had a good book to read, I might be alone but I would never be lonely.

I even remember the story she told me—how when she was little, she had caught some childhood disease and had to be quarantined (this would have been about 1918). At the end of several weeks she was all better, but her mother told her the doctor said they had to burn all her books and dolls. She couldn't care less about losing the dolls, but oh, how she cried over losing her beloved books. She handed each one over in a torrent of tears. Then, after telling this story, she would pull out the new book she had brought me from Macy's—*The Bobbsey Twins* or *Black Beauty*—and I was off and reading. My dear Aunt Ruth did this with my daughter, too, buying her a quality book each birthday and Christmas until my aunt was old and feeble. What a legacy!

—K. L.

Dads, Kids, and Time

When was the last time you and your husband had a, shall we say, lively discussion over his schedule? One episode that sticks out in my mind happened years ago, when our sons were three and six. Craig was leaving for yet another meeting, and I gave him a withering look as he headed toward the door. Our sons rushed to collect good-bye hugs while I received a duty kiss (you know the kind). Then I prepared one last parting shot, something edifying such as, "Are you sure you'll be able to find your way home later, stranger?"

Then I glanced down and saw two little noses pressed against the glass, watching their daddy leave. They waved gleefully, and I kept quiet. The thought came to me that other children could be angry with Daddy's job, but the anger would be directed toward a human boss or the company itself. In our situation, the implications were far more ominous: my sons could possibly blame the church, or even God himself. That thought has profoundly shaped the way I've tried to deal with the demands of Craig's work and its effects on our sons.

Craig and I have had MAJOR conversations about his workload, his hours at church, his periods away from us. Yet it seemed that whenever we would finally reach an agreement concerning his time and commitments, our sons would move to another stage of life, with different scheduling needs. So once again we would renegotiate and readjust. One goal has remained constant, however: determination that the ministry lifestyle not be damaging to our sons' spiritual lives.

Family time is difficult to guard, isn't it? Yet it is so important—worth the constant effort. I protected ours fiercely, and whenever Craig made a commitment to spend a day with us as a family or one-on-one with Robb or Jay, he also did his best to keep that appointment. But as you well know, ministering to people means that emergencies arise—emotional crises, hospital calls, deaths. When these unplanned contingencies ruined yet another day, our sons, though disappointed, generally reacted well when Dad explained the situation. Still, I tucked away more than one worry for those times. Did my sons carry resentment toward the church? toward God? I was not to know the answer until years later as they came to trust God with their lives. But certainly they struggled with resentment along the way as they "shared" their dad with God's people.

On the other hand, you never know what God will bring out of a situation. Read on. . . .

When We Least Expect It

The next time you wonder, *Can anything good come out of this situation?* consider what happened to us on a recent Christmas vacation.

Jay was home from college and he and Craig had planned a day together, trying out the indoor golf range, catching a "guy flick," eating out. They looked forward to both easy conversation and serious discussion. This was a day that Craig wanted to devote entirely to building his relationship with Jay.

You know what's coming. When the phone rang at an early hour, we knew it was bad news: one of the pastors on our staff team had suffered a major heart attack. Craig was needed at the hospital and, after that, at church to give the staff updates, reassurance, and comfort. We both completely understood the need, but felt heartsick for Jay. Would he understand? Or would this be yet another disappointment to add to his list as a PK?

Jay more than understood; he knew this pastor well and immediately asked if he could visit the hospital with his dad. They rushed to get ready (both donning suits and ties they'd certainly not expected to wear that day) and planted quick kisses on my cheeks as they hurried out. "Please God," I prayed, "may this day with his dad still have an impact on Jay."

After visiting the family at the hospital, Craig and Jay drove on to church so that Craig could give our staff the latest news and lead them in prayer. I wasn't at the meeting, but staff members later passed on these comments: "Craig had to stop talking several times to collect his composure; obviously, he was very emotional about this. You could feel such respect for him, and others remarked later how they appreciated his honest emotion. He was human and real, gentle and tenderhearted. To watch Jay stand by with tears in his eyes as well told me that Craig's been a father who has modeled compassion."

Any guesses about the relational area in which Jay and his dad have struggled? The same one where so many fathers and sons struggle: the expression of emotions. We could have emphasized that emotions should be appropriately expressed; we could have lectured that compassion is essential for Christians. But God's plan for the "classroom" was better. What a gift for Jay to watch his dad model each lesson.

Later, both of my guys hustled home to change clothes and "play" the remainder of the day. They got to enjoy some relaxation after all. But God had already connected them in the most unexpected way.

Every time I fret about my sons for their past, present, and future, I need to remind myself: *Their lives are tenderly cradled within God's hands*. And we mothers need to take a deep breath, open our hands, and say, "Okay, Lord. You are in control. And you will work in their lives—maybe when I least expect it."

Singing Mom Home

One of the wonderful things about worship with God's people is that you never know how immediately, how profoundly, someone may be touched by something in the service.

My mother was dying, and our family was gathered at home. On Sunday we worshiped at the church I grew up in, the church where I was loved and nurtured in the Lord many years before. We steeled our emotions so that we could listen to the service and not be touched to the point of breaking down. The choir stood to sing. I was comforted by their song, which spoke of a loving Jesus who is with us in our painful times. All we need do is truly "open our eyes" to see him walking right beside us. And then they sang of death, how God has turned that fearful ending into a glorious triumph, for in death we truly do see him.

Chosen by those in the choir who knew and loved my mother, the song was a gift to our family—a gift of love, of preparation, of hope.

—*P. J.*

Why Does This Hurt Me More Than It Hurts You?

Sooner or later, nearly everyone in the pastorate comes to a season of pain. This was ours. After diligently seeking God's will, Craig had applied for a new position, one that he seemed perfectly suited for. Receiving constant assurances that all was going well through the interview process, Craig was confident. But me? I struggled mightily. I felt like Jacob wrestling the angel.

"Why are you having such a problem with this?" Craig asked, perplexed by my emotional turmoil.

"I'm trying to be ready," I explained. "I want to accept God's yes—or no. So I'm attempting to get my emotions in line, sort of. If I prepare now for a no, then hopefully I'll be ready for it when the time comes."

"And what if God says yes?" he countered. "Won't you have wasted an awful lot of emotional energy?"

I glared at him. Craig's my number one guide spiritually, but sometimes his truths are tough to take. I also hate it when he's right.

"Carolyn, God will give you the grace to handle a no if and when it comes. Let's wait and see what he has planned, okay? Being in his will doesn't mean you have to work *now* to control your emotions for later. God doesn't expect that. And besides," he concluded practically, "it just won't work."

He was right (again), and so I put the emotional tug-of-war aside, concentrating on trusting God right now, for each today as it came. But that was only the first lesson to be learned. For, as it turned out, a resounding NO did come.

We clung to each other, searching for some form of comfort in arms that held and caressed. We poured out the pain in words and tears. And finally, we prayed, asking God to heal the hurt and show us his will.

The very next day, Craig returned wholeheartedly to life. He whistled. He smiled. He even laughed. He had processed the entire experience and was done with it. Completely. The nerve of him!

What about me? You guessed it: I was a mess.

***

For days I continued to pray, asking God to help me accept this, to release the anger that could still be rekindled whenever I remembered the cruel incident. And then one emotion began to override all the others: guilt, guilt that I had not yet worked through the entire episode.

You're nowhere near as spiritual as Craig, I berated myself. *Why can't you just let go of it?*

I prayed, floundered, and even condemned my own efforts. But ever so slowly, the emotions were not quite as intense, not as quick to rise to the surface when I prayed about our future. After many days, I was just beginning to touch the edges of peace and contentment once again when I grasped another truth: it was time to stop berating myself for who I was.

I realized then that I am not Craig. My feelings cut deeper somehow and take longer to process. I was designed this way by a Master Creator, and he does not intend for me to compare my spiritual maturity to Craig's (or anyone else's, for that matter). As long as I am seeking to know and do the Father's will, then I will not belittle my efforts nor compare them to any other's. Except Jesus Christ himself.

And by the way, didn't Jesus struggle? Alone in the garden, the shadow of the cross on the horizon, he agonized over what was to come the next day. This was not an easy acceptance. Eventually, he *decided* to do the Father's will, despite what he felt.

Maybe it's time we, following Christ's example, grasp the truth that the wrestling, the spiritual struggles, aren't mere detours along the way. Maybe it's time each of us reaffirms that there is only One in whose steps we should follow.

PART 5

Taste and See!

While they were eating, Jesus took bread and blessed it.
He broke the bread, gave it to his disciples, and said,
"Take this, and eat it. This is my body."
—Matthew 26:26

You may be a chocoholic, but give me bread any time. I love bread. Tempt me with one whiff of freshly baked bread, and I'm lost. I love to make bread, and I can't think of a better gift than a warm, homemade loaf.

So Christ's picture of himself as the Bread of Life calls powerfully to me. Bread: so elemental, so basic, so nourishing and necessary, like Jesus himself. From the time we first taste of his goodness when we commit our lives to him, he invites us to eat of him, to grow in him. His Supper, the bread and the cup, is a touchable reminder of his ultimate gift, his body, "broken for you." When he has offered and given this, can we do any less than continue to seek his nourishment? To read and pray and seek to grow? And especially when that nourishment is likened to something as delicious as bread—still warm, soft inside, crusty outside, bread? (Can you nearly taste it by now?)

I hope that as you finish this book, as you "feed" on this last section, that you'll nearly smell, feel, and taste the richness of Christ.

Consider the Finches

Have you ever really noticed birds, those bright little bits of creation? When you start watching and listening, it's amazing what you can discover. I'm an avid birdwatcher. Currently, my little friends keep me busy refilling five feeders (some for seed, others for nectars) plus a suet container. For all those efforts, I've been rewarded with the beautiful songs, antics, and glorious array of colors of finches (house, purple, and gold), orioles (I hang yet another feeder to attract them in the spring), rose-breasted and blue grosbeaks (they're much prettier than the name sounds), wrens, nuthatches, chickadees, juncos, woodpeckers (downy, hairy, and red-bellied), bluebirds, bluejays (I try to persuade these guys to chow down elsewhere), indigo buntings, sparrows, hummingbirds, and my all-time favorite, redbirds.

I can't tell you how many lessons they've taught me. One lesson came unexpectedly and has stayed with me ever since. I was standing at my kitchen sink, washing dishes, when I absentmindedly glanced out the window to see what birds might be there. It was late spring, and the male goldfinches had just shed their wintry-dull, mossy-green plumage to don their splendid yellow-gold. One brightly-hued male lit on the tree behind a feeder, nearly glowing in contrast to the emerging green leaves of the tree, and I caught my breath at the sight. Instantly, the question rushed through my mind: *Do you have any idea how gloriously beautiful you are?* And then I thought to myself, *No, you don't! You were created in splendor, but you are totally oblivious to that fact.*

I shook my head at the sad waste, at what the tiny bird could never recognize and know and appreciate. And then I thought of myself and all of us who were crafted by God. We also were created in his image, beautiful, exactly as he wanted us to be. Certainly, our worth is way beyond what a sparrow (or a goldfinch) means to him, even though he notes even a sparrow's death. In God's eyes, we are incredibly lovely and of great worth; however, like the finch, we also fail to recognize that, to accept that. We fail to view our beauty from his perspective. Could he be looking down at each of his children, admiring his creation? Is he saying to me (to *you*), at this very moment, "Do you have any idea how gloriously beautiful you are to me?" And is he sad that we also are oblivious to the splendor he has made?

Just for one moment, why not try to open your heart in a way you never have before? Allow yourself to be totally loved by God. He created you as you are. He loves you completely, just as you are. Let him wrap you in a hug. Don't you realize it? You are so beautiful!

I'm Not Laughing with Him, I'm Laughing at Him

There's nothing like laughter, is there? Silly, out-of-control giggles—how I need that nourishment for my soul! I've even heard that medical studies show a good laugh relieves stress, lowers blood pressure, helps us stay healthy. Once again scientists find that God did indeed know what he was doing when he created something!

Most of the time, my husband does his part in keeping me healthy by giving me good cause to laugh. He has a wonderful talent for bonking his head on things—fertilizer spreaders hanging in the garage, branches, canopies, car mirrors, car hoods, awnings, low-flying planes—you get the picture. He simply bangs his head on things, and after a split second of concern (honestly, I do wait a moment), I laugh. I think he does it just for me.

Then there are times when I find myself laughing at him when what I meant to do was get mad. One recent morning he was headed out, the door nearly closed

73

behind him, when I heard a faint, "Oh, by the way. I have a meeting tonight." The coward! Now, how were we to have time for a good argument when he dropped that bomb on the way out of the garage?

When I complained to his secretary, she laughed. "Carolyn," she said, "I've simply got to hand it to you. Your husband can tackle the toughest issues, confront the nastiest problems. But when it comes to facing you over guarding your time together, he turns into a shaking, quaking shadow of a husband who would rather slip out under a falling garage door and take on the whole world than stay in a confined space and face his mighty-mite wife!"

So there. I had the last laugh after all. Just another way my husband keeps me healthy and sane.

MY Kids? Rowdy?

When we moved to Colorado, we didn't know a soul. So we were very grateful when the elderly Christian woman who lived just across the street from us volunteered to baby-sit now and then for our two sons (two and five years old at the time). "Keep me in mind when you can't find anyone else," she said. "I'll be your last-minute backup."'

It wasn't long before we took her up on her offer. We had scheduled a night out and our sitter, a college student from church, couldn't come after all. So our neighbor filled in, the boys loved her, and all was wonderful. The next time, however, was a different story.

When we returned, we asked our standard questions: "How did it go? Did they behave for you?" This time our neighbor hesitated before even answering. Then she said, "Well, your sons were a bit rowdy today."

Gulp. "Rowdy? What exactly did they do?" (Did we really want to know?)

"I'd rather not say."

75

More deep breaths. "Please do."

"Well, they sprayed me with the garden hose."

Our elderly volunteer. Who baby-sat for free. Doused with ice-cold, mountain-spring-fed water. We apologized profusely, slunk with great embarrassment as we escorted her to the door, and went in search of the two little culprits to see what they had to say for themselves.

After that, we tried to stick with teenaged baby-sitters. We figured they'd simply spray 'em back.

—C. W.

Placing Our Kids on the Altar

So many pastors' wives are concerned for their children, whether they will resent the ministry, the church, and even God. I've certainly struggled with that. My sons have experienced the pain that ministry can bring; they've been targeted for blame simply because they were the ever-visible PKs. They've been uprooted from friends and moved numerous times. They were intently watched, scrutinized, and evaluated for how they reflected their dad's position. As a mom, I agonized over the damage this lifestyle was inflicting.

But know this, too. The blessings of ministry were (are) incalculable:

- Over dozens of meals in our home, they have had the privilege of personally interacting with loving, deeply spiritual saints. Will we ever fully understand what this has done for their self-esteem and interpersonal skills? what characteristics this has taught them to look for in men and women of God?

- They've learned and practiced the difference between investing in things and in people. Can we imagine what this has taught them about living simply, yet finding creative fun together?

- They caught the idea that God's opinion of them counted, not man's. What leadership qualities has this developed?

- They've seen that security rests in God. Who could imagine that a parent's losing a job would teach incredible lessons in faith and trust to all of us?

- And finally, they've watched their dad respond as a man of ethics, moral integrity, and deep spiritual maturity to countless situations. Could there be any man I would rather they emulate than their father?

Of all the gifts of nourishment that my Lord could provide, of all my desires of him, my greatest plea of him has always been that my sons grow into godly men. He has indeed fed me—but it hasn't been without struggle.

Even in the good times, most of us moms struggle with trying to be and do everything for our kids. But we all need to remember that Jesus is the Bread of Life, not us. Yes, we must and should do our part to provide an environment in which our families can grow spiritually. But then? We must be like Abraham, placing them on his altar . . . and placing them on that altar again and again and again, throughout our lives. Giving them back to God—where they belong.

Thanks . . . Again

As I was writing this book, I was ever-conscious of an overriding tension: would you feel blessed as you read some of these stories? Or would you feel pain as you heard about others' gifts? With this sensitivity in mind, I sought to steer a middle course, one that I hoped would bless, encourage, bring a bit of laughter, and awaken you to the God who can use anything to his glory.

I want you to know how much I have loved writing this for you, to you. You give so much . . . and often receive too little in return. You take your husband's and children's pain . . . and process it many times, alone. You lovingly open your hearts to others, sometimes to experience rejection or the loss of confidentiality or simply being taken for granted. And yet, in spite of so much, you offer to give yet again, you risk opening your heart once more, you smile and even laugh.

I guess you can't once be a pastor's wife without always feeling a special closeness to our unique sisterhood. Remember the story about the splendor of the goldfinch? Christ was the most glorious Gift ever given, and you, dear pastor's wife, reflect his beauty. So lift those brilliant wings, raise your voice in song, and know that you are his special gift to all those around you. You are so beautiful!

About the Author

Carolyn Williford and her husband, Craig, have been in ministry for twenty-five years. She is the author of *Devotions for Families That Can't Sit Still*, *More Devotions for Families That Can't Sit Still*, and *Jordan's Bend*, a historical novel. Craig is on the pastoral staff of The Chapel in Akron, Ohio. They have two grown sons, Robb and Jay.